PET OWNER'S GUIDE TO THE
BUDGERIGAR

Stan and Barbara Moizer

ABOUT THE AUTHORS

Stan and Barbara Moizer have been internationally respected budgerigar breeders and exhibitors for many years. At their Somerset home they keep a stud of some 350 Champion budgerigars. They have travelled extensively on lecture tours, and Stan had adjudicated at many international shows. They were both formative in setting up the World Budgerigar Organisation, which is dedicated to the promotion and welfare of the budgerigar worldwide.

In the UK, both Stan and Barbara have served on the General Council of the Budgerigar Society for many years; Stan was a former president. Barbara was editor of the magazine *The Budgerigar*. Stan also served as chairman, and both served as presidents of the Western Counties Budgerigar Society. Together, they have been responsible for a number of books on genetics and colour expectations, as well as writing *Budgerigars – a Complete Guide*, an encyclopedia of all aspects of breeding and exhibiting budgerigars.

PHOTOGRAPHY

Barbara Moizer and Amanda Bulbeck.

ACKNOWLEDGEMENTS

The authors would like to express gratitude to all who helped in the preparation of this book, including Rodney White, Sherrill Capi, 'Henry' and the White family, Steve Amos, Ron Thumwood, Arthur Bracey, Roger Stone, and the Budgerigar Society.

Published by Ringpress Books,
Vincent Lane, Dorking, Surrey,
RH4 3YX, England.

First published 1997
© Interpet Publishing. All rights reserved

ISBN 1 86054 038 4

Printed in Hong Kong through Printworks Int. Ltd.

CONTENTS

Introducing Budgerigars

Today budgerigars are among the most popular of pet birds, but, in fact, they are relative newcomers – in 1840 they were unknown outside their native home, Australia. A naturalist named John Gould brought the first pair to England from Australia, and everyone who saw them was fascinated by the tiny parrots. Dealers saw the potential and arranged with sailors to bring in cages full of budgerigars.

BIG PROFITS

The prices charged were exorbitant, and only the very rich could afford them. With such profits to be made, merchants throughout Europe soon began importing them on a much larger scale. Hundreds of thousands started flooding into Europe – until the Australian government put a ban on the export of parakeets. Today, budgerigars are bred from existing stock and they are no longer imported from their native home.

WHAT'S IN A NAME?

When Captain James Cook discovered Australia in 1770, one of the wonders reported by the sailors was the immense flocks of pretty green birds. They flew in flocks so large that, as they passed, they blotted out the sun for miles and the land grew dark. When they alighted on the branches of dead trees, their brilliant green plumage gave the impression that the tree had suddenly come back to life and was covered with leaves.

When the early settlers came across the Aborigines, they asked them, in sign language, what these birds were called. The Aborigines repeated, again and again, something which sounded like "betchery-gah". The settlers presumed that this was the name of the bird and named it 'Budgerigar'. Many years later, when linguists translated the Aborigine language, they discovered that the word actually meant 'good to eat'!

THE FIRST IMPORTS

The native budgies, and all the early imported budgies, were of the light-green variety. They had green wings with black markings, and a yellow head and body. They were, and still are, much smaller than the pet budgies we see today. They measured only four inches from head to the tip of the tail, compared with exhibition budgerigars who can measure as much as ten inches in length.

The owners of the newly-imported budgies, mostly zoos, experimented with breeding them. They discovered that in the wild, the birds built their nests in holes in rotting tree branches, hollowing out a dark space where the hen could lay her eggs and rear her chicks in safety. The nearest equivalent the early breeders could find was a coconut shell with an entrance hole drilled into it. The accommodating little birds, accepted this new form of nest, and soon proliferated.

NEW COLOURS

When the first colour mutation occurred in 1870 in Belgium, it caused a sensation among the new budgie breeders. The bird was pure yellow all over, no black markings, and it had red eyes. Its owner thought that he would make a fortune breeding these beautiful new birds, but, sadly, no more appeared. However, another variety did appear and was successfully bred. This was also yellow, but it had pale markings on its wings and the eyes were black.

At the beginning of the 20th century, rumours began to circulate that someone had bred an incredibly beautiful budgerigar with a smooth blue body, blue wings with black markings and a pure-white face. The budgerigar

This little wild budgie (pictured left), rescued by an Australian breeder, shows the amazing difference in size between the original wild birds introduced into the UK, and the present-day domestic budgie.

A lutino is all-yellow with red eyes.

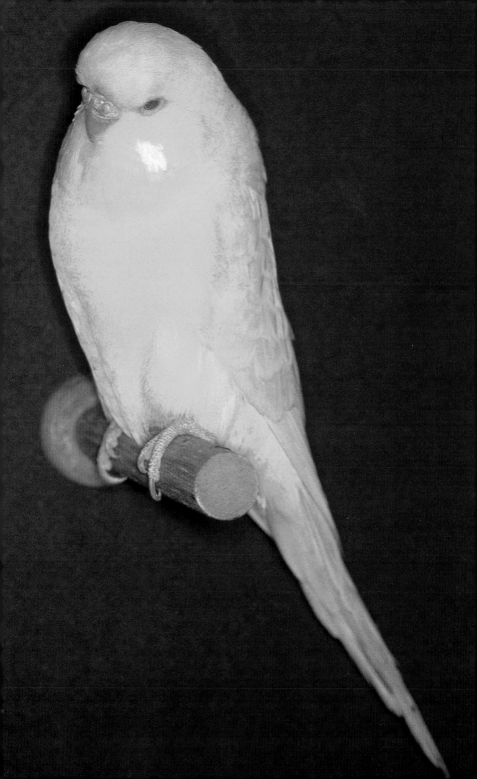

fraternity, which included King George V, the Marquess of Tavistock and other members of the British aristocracy, endeavoured to discover who the breeder was and where he lived.

However, it was not until 1910 that the first sky-blue birds were shown at a bird show at the Horticultural Hall, London – and they caused a sensation. The Royal House of Japan had become interested in budgerigars, and was reputed to have paid an astronomical sum for a pair of these blue birds (which are so common today). Other members of the Japanese nobility started the fashion of giving these beautiful blue-and-white budgies as love tokens – and so those first breeders, who were able to produce the new, blue mutation, became rich on the proceeds.

A light-green dominant pied.

THE FANCY GROWS

At this time, the budgerigar fancy still consisted of the privileged few. In the UK, an exclusive club, named the Budgerigar Club, was formed in 1925. King George V was asked to become its patron in 1930; he agreed but insisted that it should be renamed the Budgerigar Society, the name by which it is still known today. The royal tradition of keeping a flock of budgerigars is still continued today with Queen Elizabeth II and the Queen Mother keeping well-known studs.

As more and more budgies were bred, new mutations followed each other. The 'all-yellow birds with red eyes', which we now know as lutinos, reappeared, along with all-white albinos, and birds with various colour patches, called pieds. Soon the huge variety of colours and patterns which we know today was established, and the hobby of breeding budgerigars passed out of the hands of the rich and aristocratic into the hands of ordinary people.

Nowadays, anyone requiring an affectionate and absorbing pet, can buy a budgie quite cheaply from a pet store or a breeder, choosing the sex and colours

The all-white albino.

reached the grand old age of twenty or more!

Budgies make great pets because:

- They are easy to care for.
- They do not need to be taken for walks.
- Budgie feathers are usually tolerated by people with fur allergies.
- They take up very little room.
- They can learn to talk.
- They are attractive to look at.
- They are cheeky and inquisitive, making them fun to own.
- The above reasons make them perfect pets for the elderly.
- These reasons, plus the fact that a budgie can learn to talk, make them perfect pets for young and old alike.

GOING AWAY

When budgie owners are going away on holiday, it is usually not difficult to find someone who will take in a house guest which is so easy to look after.

However, full instructions should be given to the foster hosts to ensure that the cage is sited properly, and feeding and watering carried out in accordance with the bird's regular routine.

(there are over 60 different colours and varieties) they would like.

THE IDEAL PET

Budgerigars make ideal pets. Even when the landlord has a 'no pets' rule, budgies are usually allowed. They are the most companionable of birds, living for around eight years – although some have

Budgies are easy to transport.

Showing budgies is an absorbing hobby.

The top breeders exhibit budgies of many different varieties. This is a lacewing. It look similar to the all-yellow lutino, but it has faint markings on the wings and spots.

THERAPY PETS

The therapeutic value of keeping budgerigars is a well-known medical fact – having companionship and someone to talk to is a boon for a lonely person. On doctors' orders, aviaries and·stock cages of budgies have been set up in many residential homes for the elderly and in long-stay hospitals.

There are also many cases of prisoners being allowed to keep budgies in their cells or in prison corridors. Perhaps the best known example of this in the UK is Broadmoor Prison for the criminally insane. In 1956, the humane and understanding superintendent gave permission to a prisoner to build and stock an aviary of budgerigars and he began to breed them. Other patients heard about them, went to see them and wanted budgies of their own.

Soon the hobby of budgerigar breeding became endemic. There were budgies in the wards, the galleries, the day-rooms, and even some flying free in corridors. Far from upsetting the doctors and staff, it was found that the hobby kept even the most disturbed patients happier, healthier and easier to control. The inmates corresponded with the Budgerigar Society who put them in touch with their local clubs. Soon they were receiving visits from many famous speakers from all over the country.

EXHIBITING BUDGIES

When you have bred a few budgies, you may join your local cage bird or budgerigar society – there are over 1,000 clubs in the UK, and there is widespread interest in most other countries. Details of addresses and meeting places can usually be obtained from your local library or from a local newspaper. Here you will meet other breeders and learn about shows being held in your area.

For new breeders, it is a temptation to enter their birds in a show and, if it is a small show such as a club members' show it is possible that one or two prize cards will be won – mostly in classes with small entries. Unfortunately, newcomers can be easily disillusioned when going on to enter a larger show where their entries may end up at the bottom of every class. As a new breeder, it is natural to think that your birds are just as good as any others. However, the wise breeder will start going to shows as a spectator and will ask many questions.

WHAT MAKES A WINNER?

What makes a budgerigar into a winning specimen is complicated and will take a while to learn. So many aspects of the bird have to be taken into consideration. The overall length is important (the ideal length is 21 cms, 8½ inches), a wide face is needed, height over the cere, deportment, the way the wings are carried. All these points are taken into consideration – even the shape, size and positioning of the spots will be assessed. It is a learning curve which every new breeder must go through. The number of different classes can also be daunting. In most Championship shows there are over 200 classes for budgies. Each colour, through all the different varieties, has four or five different classes, categorised into: Beginner, Novice, Intermediate and Champion, plus extra classes for Juniors.

In the UK, once a breeder has decided to become an exhibitor, he or she should become a member of the Budgerigar Society. For an annual fee, the member receives a bi-monthly, coloured magazine filled with advice and news of shows and other activities of the various area societies. Most importantly, the new member is issued with a closed, coded ring number which will be exclusive to him, worldwide. This number will appear on leg rings, which should be put on the birds when they are 7-10 days old and which cannot be removed unless cut off. It is a lifelong identification for an owner's birds. Other countries have a similar system of registration, as well as official budgerigar organisations.

NEW HORIZONS

Anyone who does decide to become a budgerigar fancier will find that he has joined a world where friendship and camaraderie rule. From one end of the country to the other, the budgie fancier can wander into one of the thousands of shows which are held and be in the company of friendly people who speak a common language – all about budgies. After a short time, you will recognise the regulars and be greeted by them. Some of the shows become meeting places for friends who see each other only once or twice a year at particular shows. But they know that, should they need assistance, it will be given gladly.

We have travelled all over the world judging budgies, giving lectures and making friends in Canada, the USA, Brazil, Eire, Europe and Australia. There seems to be no end to the adventures of a budgie fancier. The competitive breeders will find an unbelievable selection of cups and trophies, cash and other prizes which are offered to successful breeders of all the different varieties of budgerigars. It is a hobby for all ages. There are classes for Juniors, and there are Champion breeders of eighty years of age and more, still enjoying every moment of their lives.

Choosing A Budgerigar

Before you buy your pet, it is best to consider whether you and your family have the time to spend playing with it and talking to it. Budgerigars are sociable creatures and are not used to being alone. If the bird is likely to be left on its own for long periods, it is kinder to buy two budgies so that they will have each other to play with. A lone budgie will adopt its owner as its family. It will be happiest when it is allowed out of its cage and can sit on a finger, a shoulder, a head, or on some other favourite perch. A budgie will not be happy alone in a cage, left to its own devices.

If you particularly want a budgie which will talk, then it is necessary to buy a single bird because, when there is more than one, they talk to each other in 'Budgie speak', and do not learn our language. It is only when a budgie is kept alone and spoken to often, that it will learn to mimic its owner.

The next thing to decide is the colour and sex you would prefer. There is a fantastic choice of colours and varieties. Some of these are more difficult to obtain than others, but if your local pet shop cannot help, the staff will probably know of another retail source, or they may know of a local breeder. In the UK, the Budgerigar Society has a Pet Owner's Club which keeps a list of registered breeders. These breeders will assist newcomers buying budgies for the first time, and will give any other advice that is required. Other countries have similar organisations that will provide advice and information for the novice budgie owner.

ASSESSING AGE

The age of the bird is very important for pets, because birds that are over three or four months old are much more difficult to finger-train and you will find it hard to teach them to talk. Blue or

A close-up of the head bars of a baby sky-blue cock. At about three months old these bars moult out and the head becomes pure white. Note the pale colouring of the cere, which makes sexing babies difficult.

MALE OR FEMALE?

The cere of the bird tells you its sex but, unfortunately, when the bird is very young, the cere is not fully coloured. The cere is the hard patch above the beak which has the two nostril holes in it. In an adult cock it is blue, and in an adult hen it is brown. When the birds are young, the blue of the cock is more of a pink, purplish

green series birds under three months old have bars of black feathers across the top of their heads, and if you look at the eyes, they are solid black, with no white iris rings. Another clue to age is the throat spots. Adult birds have large, well-defined black spots around the front of the throat. In baby birds there are usually multiple black spots or flecks of black.

The brown cere of this light-green hen clearly shows the difference from the blue of the cock's cere.

colour, and the brown of the hen is a bluish-white. Both sexes can be taught to speak but, in general, the males are more friendly than the females, although this is not always the case.

SIGNS OF A HEALTHY BIRD

Check to see that the bird you buy is healthy. If a budgie has been left in a draught it can catch a cold, or if it has been kept in close proximity to a sick bird, it can catch whatever that bird was suffering from. A healthy budgie has bright and alert eyes, its feathers are held close to its body – not all fluffed up – and the vent is clean and dry. If the budgie is caged alone, check on the droppings; they should be solid, and black and white in colour. Soft, spreading or light-coloured droppings usually denote some illness, as do dull, watery eyes, or loose, ruffled, or untidy feathers. Never buy a budgie with running eyes or a wet, green, dirty vent.

If you know an experienced budgie breeder, it would be a good idea to ask him or her to go with you to the pet shop to ensure that you choose the sex you want, and to check that the birds are fit and healthy.

A healthy budgie should appear bright and alert, with its feathers held tightly to its body.

COLOURS AND VARIETIES
BASIC VARIETIES

The basic colours of budgerigars are blue and green, but each of the colours comes in three shades. There is sky–blue (the lightest shade), cobalt blue (the middle shade), and mauve (the darkest shade). In the green series there is light green, dark green (this is the middle shade) and olive green. These six colours come in the

The wing of a spangle budgie showing how the markings differ from the norm.

normal variety, where the face is white and the body is a solid colour of blue in the blue series, and the face is yellow and the body a solid colour of green in the green series. In both, the wings are marked with wavy, black bars.

OPALINE

All of these six colours can be found in the opaline variety. These birds are an opalescent glowing colour, and the body colour is more pronounced on the wing.

CINNAMON

In the cinnamon variety, the six colours are modified by the addition of a cinnamon shade.

This causes the body colour to become a more delicate shade, and all the black markings in the wings become brown.

GREY

The addition of grey to the basic colours has a strange effect. In the green series, the green becomes almost a khaki shade, while in the blue series, the grey factor covers up all the blue and the bird is visually light, mid or dark grey.

PIED VARIETIES

The pied variety includes the most colourful birds – and there are different kinds of pieds to add to the choice available.

AUSTRALIAN PIED

The Australian pieds come in any of the six basic colours, or in grey, but they differ from the normals because they have irregular patches of yellow in their bodies in the green birds, and irregular patches of white in the blue birds. They often have a little patch of the opposite colour from the body just on top of their heads, and there can be irregular patches of colour or clear-coloured feathers among the black bars of the wings.

RECESSIVE PIED (Harlequin)

The recessive pieds are very popular as pets because they are the most colourful of all the varieties. The general colour of the body is either bright, grass green or azure blue in the light series, but they are covered in irregular patches of blue and white or green and yellow. The wings are almost all clear colour, except for a few patches of black undulations or polka dots. The most beautiful are the violet recessive pieds, with mixed patches of deep violet and white.

VIOLET

The violet variety is very much

Yellow-faced Mauve.

like the blue, except that the shade is a rich violet. This variety is quite rare.

YELLOW-FACED

Another variation is the yellow-faced variety. Here the blue bird has a yellow face and head and, once again, this is also available in the pied variety – which makes a very colourful bird.

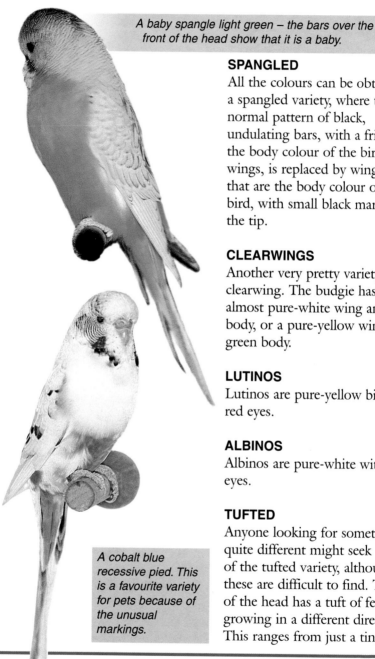

A baby spangle light green – the bars over the front of the head show that it is a baby.

A cobalt blue recessive pied. This is a favourite variety for pets because of the unusual markings.

SPANGLED

All the colours can be obtained in a spangled variety, where the normal pattern of black, undulating bars, with a fringe of the body colour of the bird on the wings, is replaced by wing feathers that are the body colour of the bird, with small black marks on the tip.

CLEARWINGS

Another very pretty variety is the clearwing. The budgie has an almost pure-white wing and a blue body, or a pure-yellow wing and a green body.

LUTINOS

Lutinos are pure-yellow birds with red eyes.

ALBINOS

Albinos are pure-white with red eyes.

TUFTED

Anyone looking for something quite different might seek a budgie of the tufted variety, although these are difficult to find. The top of the head has a tuft of feathers growing in a different direction. This ranges from just a tiny tuft growing wrongly, a version where half the head feathers spread out, to a full crown, which gives the impression of a budgie with a fringe around its head. This variety, like most of the others, can be obtained in all the different colours.

There are even more varieties available, but it would be very hard to track these down unless you were involved in the budgie-breeding fancy.

For more information contact:
UK: The Budgerigar Society, 49-53 Hazelwood Road, Northampton, NN1 1LG.

USA: American Budgerigar Society, 617 n. 7th Street, Grimes, Iowa, 5011.

3

Buying Equipment

When you buy your first budgie, you will want to make its home as comfortable as possible. There are some necessities, and several other extras which will ensure that your budgie feels happy and comfortable in his new surroundings. There are also a number of items which will make life easier for you – like a base cover and a bath. Most of the equipment required is not very expensive, and will last a lifetime.

CHOOSING THE CAGE

If you do not already have a budgie cage, you need to choose one at the same time as you buy your birds. The most important thing to remember is that budgies fly from side to side – not upwards. However attractive the very tall cylindrical cages appear to you, the budgie is not going to appreciate a cage where there is no room to fly back and forth, from perch to perch. The wider the cage the better, especially if you are

A fully-equipped cage.

buying several birds which will be expected to spend long periods of time together without being let out. The ideal size for a single bird would be at least 45cm x 30cm x 30cm and approximately (50cm x 36cm x 36cm) for two to four birds.

SITING THE CAGE

The location of the cage must be carefully considered. Budgies are generally healthy little creatures, but they cannot stand draughts, so make certain that the cage is sited several feet above the ground, and away from doors and windows. If you have a cat, make sure that it cannot jump on to the cage – this could, literally, frighten a bird to death. The cage must also be sited away from direct sunlight as this can cause suffering, especially in sunny weather.

ACCESSORIES

You will need a few accessories to go with your cage.

WATER-DRINKERS

Water-drinkers are a necessity. There are several different types to choose from. The most popular is the fountain type; this consists of a clear, plastic tube with an open end. When this is filled, a cap with a drinking spout is fitted and the fountain is turned upside down. The force of gravity fills the drinking spout meaning that water is always available to the birds. Care must be taken not to fit the cap with the cut-out piece meeting the cut-out on the

tube, otherwise the water will run out as it is fitted to the cage, leaving the bird with only the few drops left in the spout. The tube clips on to the cage, and so the level of water is always visible. Another advantage is that the birds cannot use it as a bath, and splash the water around.

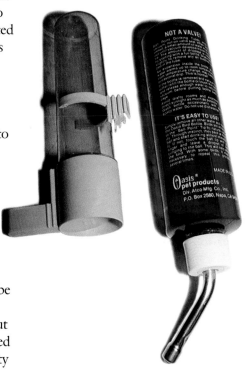

Two types of water-drinker. The type on the right is more hygienic as dropping cannot fall into the water-spout.

Never use the drinking fountain for seed. Seed can jam up in the tube so that there are only a few grains in the base for the bird to eat. Tragically, there have been many instances of budgies starving to death, while it appeared that they had a full tube of seed.

The other recommended water container is the type that is usually sold for hamsters. This time the tube is opaque, which prevents the formation of green algae on the inside of the tube. The base of the tube has a narrow, metal tube with a valve on the end. The birds very quickly learn that when they press the valve, it delivers a drop of water.

FOOD CONTAINER

Seed should always be given in an open container. These are usually part of the fittings of the cage. If they are not, care should be taken to ensure that feeding dishes are not situated under a perch, where they could be fouled by droppings. A very good feeding dish is the type made of glazed pottery or china, with a hood shape, which just covers the top and keeps any droppings from getting in.

PERCHES

A set of perches usually comes with the cage. These are generally made of round or oval-shaped dowelling, and they are all identical. However, this is not suitable for the health and well-being of your budgie, who needs different widths and shapes to cling to and to land upon. If you watch your budgie, you will see that it holds tightly to the perch to balance, and every time it hops from perch to perch, it lands on the same part of the foot. If it lands on an identical perch, it will land on the same part of its foot every time, and this can cause corns to develop. As you can imagine, these can be very painful if they are landed on with force.

The cage will need perches. Sand can be used to cover the floor of the cage, or you can use disposable sandpaper.

The budgie could also develop bumble foot. This is a bacterial infection of the foot which causes it to become swollen and tender – and it will need the attention of a vet.

When the feet are given perches of different width and shape, the feet stay healthy, and for the outlay of very little money, you will have a happy, corn-free budgie. This can be done by simply replacing one or more of the round perches with timber $\frac{1}{2}$ in x $\frac{5}{8}$ in. If you have fruit trees in the garden, a thin branch can be used as a perch – budgies love to strip the bark. A branch from a eucalyptus tree is also suitable, but be careful not to use any type of tree because some are poisonous.

FLOOR COVERING

The floor of the cage will need some sort of cover to make it easy

Budgies require different widths of perches – the branches of fruit trees are recommended.

to clean. Some budgie keepers cut sheets of thick plastic material which they can pull out and wash, others use sheets of newspaper which they can change frequently. The disadvantage of this is that budgies love to tear paper into shreds, and shredded paper can make a lot of mess. Ready-made sand sheets are available in most pet shops. These are easy to change, and the budgies like them because they can scratch away at them and keep their claws in trim.

BASE COVER

This is a very useful accessory to buy when you purchase your cage. These are generally made in plastic or nylon material which is easily washed. Budgies, especially babies, love to scratch and scatter seed. They are adept at scattering it over a wide distance, so a base cover will save a great deal of cleaning up and vacuuming. We find that a cover, or a very wide tray, is essential to keep the peace in a house.

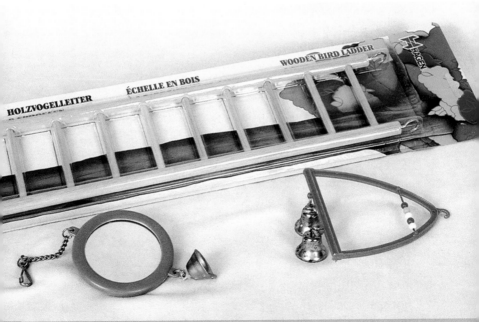

Budgies appreciate a variety of toys. Mirrors, bells and ladders are favourites.

LANDING PLATFORM

This is a useful addition once you begin to let your pet out of the cage. This fits on to the doorway of the cage and enables the budgie to fly back into its cage without difficulty. They are inexpensive but very useful.

TOYS AND GAMES

Budgies will amuse themselves for hours with simple toys, but before you buy any, check them just as carefully as you would check toys for children. Do not clutter up the cage with so many toys that they become a danger, or prevent free movement in the cage. Put in just one or two toys at a time, changing them periodically.

MIRROR

This is a piece of equipment that you should buy at the same time as your bird. It is likely that you will be taking your budgie away from all its companions, and a mirror will help to stop it from feeling lonely until it gets used to you and its new family. The best choice of mirror is one made from polished steel, because if it is dropped or pulled off in play, it will not shatter, leaving minute slivers of glass which could be picked up by the budgie.

Budgies are surprisingly agile, and will enjoy playing on a swing.

You will find that the purchase of a mirror will be worth its weight in gold as you watch your budgie play with, feed, and talk to its mirror.

BELLS

You can buy a bell for your

budgies, or sometimes a mirror will have a bell attached. This toy can be fun for both you and your budgie, as you can easily train the bird to ring the bell. This can be used as a signal – when the budgie wants to come out of the cage, for example.

Check that the clapper of the bell is very firmly fixed. A budgie can try to swallow a tiny clapper or a loose bead and choke itself, just as easily as a child can. Bear in mind that anything with a piece of loose wire hanging out can cause damage to claws, eyes or skin.

LADDER

Budgies love to run up and down ladders, but check that the spaces between the runs are not so narrow that the budgie could trap its head, or its body.

BATH-TIME

A favourite budgie toy is a mirror at the bottom of a shallow dish that is filled with water. Make sure the water is only about one inch in depth. Budgies love to splash about in the water – but splash is

An atomiser can be used for spraying your budgie in hot weather.

the operative word. The best plan is to position the cage on a wide piece of newspaper or an old cloth before you put in the water. A budgie can splash over quite a wide radius, and, without some form of protection, wet furniture or carpets are likely to result.

Pet shops sell ready-made baths which fit on to the cage entrance. These are enclosed on three sides, which means that only the cage gets wet. Budgies are often afraid of this type of bath to begin with, and your budgie may need to be coaxed to use it.

The best method is to select a favourite treat, like a piece of millet spray, a piece of apple or orange, or a few sprays of chickweed, and put the food at the furthest end from the cage entrance. This will help to tempt the budgie into the cage, even though it is worried about the new bath. Once the budgie has overcome its initial nervousness, it will hop in the moment the bath is fixed to the cage.

ATOMISER

Budgies also like a shower in hot weather. You can buy an atomiser, such as the type used for spraying plants, and fill it with lukewarm water. Give your budgie a gentle spraying, and you will be delighted to see how much the bird enjoys it.

DOLLS

There is a type of doll which has a wider round bottom than top, so that it always rights itself when pushed over. Your budgie will enjoy trying to make it lie down. But remember, your budgie thinks of you as its companion, and will expect you to join in its games. The budgie will throw the doll, or anything else, from the top of the cage, and your job is to pick it up and put it back so that it can throw it off again – and so the game continues. Budgies certainly teach you patience!

HOMEMADE TOYS

If shop-bought toys are not available, homemade toys will be enjoyed just as much. A few empty cotton reels, strung on a piece of string, will be dragged around and thrown over with the greatest of enjoyment. As chewing the string, or anything else, is all part of the fun, you will need to renew it fairly frequently.

Another source of fun is a narrow tray, with a few glass marbles As glass marbles are reasonably heavy, and the tray has a lip which keeps them in place, the budgie has quite a struggle to heave them over the top and on to the floor of the cage – but heave them he does and, yes, your task is to pick them all up. This is one of the occasions when the budgie may ring his bell, telling you that he has succeeded in pushing all the marbles off and needs a refill.

GOODNIGHT BUDGIE!

Sometimes budgies can become a real nuisance when they want to play with bells and tweet, and you need some peace and quiet. Covering the cage with an opaque cover will usually solve this problem, as the budgie will think it is night-time and will go to sleep.

THE GARDEN AVIARY

Many people prefer to keep their birds in a garden aviary. Although planning permission is not normally required for building a

garden aviary, it is wise to check first with neighbours to be certain there will be no objection to the tweeting of the budgies. On some housing developments there are restrictions regarding the keeping of pets. It is important to solve any potential problems before going to the trouble and expense of building and stocking your own aviary. A garden aviary can be a source of unending pleasure to bird lovers as they sit and watch the antics of budgies at play. It can become the focal point of a garden which can prove popular with family, visitors and neighbours alike.

BUILD YOUR OWN AVIARY

The simplest and most basic type of garden aviary, which could be built for a small outlay, consists of an open flight, a rigid framework covered with wire netting or weldmesh, and secure sleeping quarters. If possible, the aviary

35

should have a sound concrete base, or an easier solution is to purchase concrete paving slabs of convenient sizes. The base should be built with a slight slope to allow the rain to run off. If, for some reason, it is not possible to construct a concrete base, then the aviary must be pegged very firmly to the ground to ensure that, even in the worst storm, it could not be blown over.

A simple method of constructing the sleeping quarters is to make a four-sided wooden box, with a window in the rear wall. This will allow light into the quarters so that you will be able to see the birds without opening the door. The front, which faces into the flight, is made into an opening door to facilitate cleaning.

You will need to cut two entrance holes into the door, about 10 cm (5 ins) in diameter to allow the birds to enter and leave

A garden aviary can be built to meet your own requirements.

the sleeping quarters. Make sure the edges of the holes are smooth so that the birds do not injure themselves.

Inside the sleeping quarters, two or three perches should be fitted firmly, lengthways. To facilitate cleaning, sawdust or shavings can be sprinkled on the floor of the sleeping quarters, and the floor should be scraped, washed and disinfected weekly. If the floor of the aviary is concrete, it is easier to clean – and nicer to look at – if a liberal covering of coarse sand or stone chippings is spread over it. The sand must first be washed clean of salt.

THE FOCAL POINT

Up to 25 birds can be comfortably housed in a flight 2–2.5m long, a minimum of 1m wide, and 2m high. The framework can be made from 5 x 5cm timber, or from suitable hard, plastic tubing. If timber is to be used, it must be treated with a non-toxic wood preservative prior to fitting the wire netting.

Both top and sides of the framework should be totally covered with heavy, small-gauge wire netting or weldmesh to prevent the birds from escaping, and to protect them from cats,

children and vermin. All the wire netting should be painted with black bitumastic paint, both inside and out, as a preservative. The roof should be covered with a solid opaque material to give the birds shelter from the sun and rain. This can be boarded and felted, or covered with fibreglass sheeting or something similar.

The flight area needs to be covered with strong, corrugated, well-secured plastic sheeting to protect the budgerigars from the droppings of wild birds who could be carrying infection, especially in their droppings. With birds in a garden aviary it is particularly important to watch very carefully for any signs of illness or infestation.

GROUND COVER

If a concrete base has not been built, it is best to have an earth floor and to fork over the ground lightly every so often, otherwise the ground under the perches becomes soured with droppings. When the soil is forked over, the birds like to break it up, looking for grubs, insects and natural minerals.

Grass is not a good floor because the birds would quickly eat it, leaving ground which would be hard to fork over. For the same reason, it is not a good idea to plant any type of plant or tree inside the flight, because the budgies would very quickly strip it of every leaf and bud – and remember, some plants are poisonous.

However, budgies do appreciate branches pruned from apple, pear or plum trees, just for them to play with. They will strip off the leaves and bark and will play with them for hours. Then they will use the bare twigs as perches or playthings.

SAFETY DOOR

For access to the flight and, through that, to the sleeping quarters, a safety door or porch is necessary. This consists of a PVC tube or timber frame extending out a few feet from the entrance door of the aviary, covered with wire mesh. It has a door, preferably opening inwards, which can also be made of a frame covered with netting or weldmesh.

PRESERVING GOOD RELATIONS

If you do not wish to breed birds, you must never put anything in the aviary that resembles a nesting box, otherwise this could cause jealousy and fighting among the hens. They would fight for the opportunity of breeding – and fighting hens can be quite vicious. In fact, if the garden aviary is wanted just for the joy of watching the budgies at play, it is wiser to limit the birds to one sex, preferably males.

READY-MADE AVIARIES

There are many ready-made aviaries on the market, some of them quite elaborate and ornate, but they will all need the same firm concrete base and the same amount of care and cleaning. When choosing an aviary, the welfare of the birds must be the main consideration, so check that the aviary you choose has the basic facilities of the simple aviary described above.

FOLLOW THE SAME ROUTINE

Remember, once you have built and stocked your aviary, you must carry out all the regular tasks which have been recommended for one pet bird. There are large seed and water containers suitable for aviaries, which are available in most pet stores. Seed dishes must have the husks blown off and be topped up daily. Grit dishes must be inspected, and any grit which

A garden aviary will give you the opportunity to keep many more birds, and they will enjoy far greater freedom.

has been ground to dust should be discarded. Water must be changed daily. When you are keeping a number of birds in a relatively confined space, hygiene is of the utmost importance.

SECURITY

Security must be a top priority. When a bird escapes from an aviary it will fly for long distances in panic, and then cannot find its way back home. Sadly, escaped budgies often die of starvation because seed, their natural food, is seldom available – and they are not used to trying to skirmish for scraps among a flock of quarrelling garden birds.

4 Caring For Your Budgie

A budgie's natural diet is seeding grasses. In Australia, throughout the wet summer season, seeding grasses are prolific, and this is the time that budgies build their nests and breed. When the rains fall, the birds have to survive on the dried ripe seeds which have fallen, plus any grubs which they can find in the rotted trees. They also like to eat the leaves of eucalyptus trees, which are native to Australia.

Our pet budgies love seeding grasses too, but, unfortunately, much of our grassland is contaminated by pesticides, or animal droppings and urine, making it too dangerous to gather wild grasses. The commercial seed-packers have, therefore, incorporated various minerals and vitamins into their products to make them as near to the natural food as possible.

SEEDS

There are a number of pre-packed mixed seeds for budgies, and, if you have only one or two birds, this will be the best choice. If you have a number of birds in a garden aviary, or if you start breeding budgies, then it is best to feed seed in separate dishes: one of best-quality canary seed, and another of mixed millets. (For further advice on feeding breeding budgies see Chapter Seven).

Pre-packed budgie seed.

Budgies love millet – but it must be rationed.

MILLET
Budgies love millet sprays, but you have to ration them because millet is fattening and if allowed, the birds would eat it all the time instead of their ordinary seed. For one budgie in a cage, a single spray a week is plenty.

GRIT
Budgies need grit to digest their food. Birds

Grit is an essential part of the diet.

have no teeth and so they do not chew the seeds they eat, but swallow them whole. They start by taking off the outside husk and discarding it. Once swallowed, the seed eventually passes into the gizzard, which is like a grinding machine, grinding the seed so that it can be absorbed by the body. However, in order to function, the gizzard needs grit. There are a number of forms of grit available in packets, or it can be bought loose. Make sure that the type you choose is fairly coarse; grit as fine as sand is of little use to birds. Grit should always be given in a separate dish.

TREATS FOR BUDGIES
Budgies like fruit and greenfood, but this must be given in moderation. They will eat a segment of sweet apple or orange if it is stuck through the bars of the cage. They also love chickweed, especially fresh wet chickweed, which they can roll in as well as eat. When this is not available, they will accept lettuce and green salad ingredients.

When giving any form of greenfood it is essential to check that this has not been contaminated by sprays or fouled by animal urine. For just one or two budgies, the best plan is to grow a little greenfood in a pot in the house (or in the greenhouse), so you can be certain that it is 100 per cent clean. Pet shops sell small, ready-planted pots of seed that just need watering to start them growing. These can be attached to a cage, and the grass and greenfood grows through the bars – but not for long – because it is quickly eaten by the budgies. Any greenfood not eaten at the end of a day should be removed and thrown away, otherwise it could go stale and cause tummy upsets.

Greenfood can be given in moderation.

MINERALS

Another extra, appreciated by budgies, is an iodine block. Most of the mineral requirements of a budgie are available in its normal food, but iodine is an exception. This can be supplied by little pink-coloured blocks sold by pet shops. They have a flexible metal fastener to hook on to the cage.

CUTTLE-FISH

Cuttle-fish bone is a vital source of calcium, and is something else that budgies love to scratch to pieces. Cuttle-fish is readily available in pet shops.

The cage will need to be cleaned thoroughly once a week.

GENERAL CARE

Looking after your budgie is very little trouble. However, it is best to work to a regular routine so that you do not forget to do any of the small tasks.

DAILY TASKS

WATER

Water should be changed every day and the water fountain, or any other water container, should be washed out, preferably using a disinfectant suitable for baby bottles.

SEED POTS

The seed pot must be blown off every day. A budgie takes off the husk before it eats its seed, and the husk is usually left in the seed pot. This means that the seed pot often looks full, when there are only a few seeds left in it. Every day, the seed pots should be taken outside, all the husk blown off, and then refilled with fresh seed.

WEEKLY TASKS

Every week it is necessary to check the grit pot to make sure that it has not all been ground up to dust, or to very fine particles. If it has, the waste material needs to be discarded and the pot must be refilled with fresh grit.

CLEANING

All the containers should be washed and disinfected. This also applies to the perches. If the perches have been fouled with droppings, they should be scraped clean before being washed and disinfected. Finally, the sand sheet or whatever floor covering you use, should be changed.

OCCASIONAL TASKS

BEAK AND CLAWS

Occasionally, usually as a budgie gets older, the claws or the beak grow too long. Overgrown claws

If claws grow too long, they will need to be cut with nail-clippers.

can make it difficult or painful for the bird to perch properly, and so they must be attended to. Cutting the nails is quite a simple procedure, but unless you are experienced, it is best to have someone to hold the bird for you.

You need a sharp, strong pair of nail-clippers. The first step is to hold the bird up to the light so that you can see the blood vessels in the claws. You will see that they end about 1/8 inch from the end of the claw. If the claw is very long, the distance from the blood vessels to the end of the claw may

be greater. The aim is to cut the claw just below the blood vessels. If you go any further, you will cut into the blood supply. It is best to clip a little at a time, holding the budgie up to the light after each snip to make sure that you are not cutting too far up the claw. As long as you are cutting the claw – not the blood vessel – it is not at all painful for the bird. It is just the same as cutting your own nails.

The same procedure applies to cutting the beak. If the beak becomes overgrown – and this happens only on very rare occasions – it can interfere with the way the budgie eats. Although the method of cutting the beak is the same as for the claws, it is better to ask an experienced breeder or a vet to do the job. This is because the shape needs to be maintained, and so the snipping has to follow the contours of the beak.

LEG RINGS
Rings, which can be so useful in tracing a bird or its breeder, can also cause a problem. A tiny piece of grit or sand can become wedged between the ring and the budgie's leg. This causes irritation, and, in its attempts to dislodge it,

the budgie can cause an abrasion of the skin. This, in turn, can cause infection and swelling. The ring can become impacted and even cut off the blood supply.

To avoid this happening, every time you catch your budgie to clean its cage, or for any other reason, check that the ring can be moved freely around the leg. If it is immovable, particularly if there is any swelling, it should be cut off immediately. A vet or an experienced breeder will do this for you.

UNDERSTANDING YOUR BUDGIE

First-time owners of budgerigars often become concerned about behaviour which is, in fact, entirely natural.

ON ONE LEG

A healthy budgie quite frequently stands on one leg, tucking the other up under its body. When it goes to sleep, the budgie stands on one leg and tucks its head under its wing.

REGURGITATING

A budgie will often regurgitate seed and feed another bird in the cage. It may feed its own reflection in the mirror, or it may simply let the regurgitated seed fall to the floor. This is part of breeding behaviour, and does not indicate ill health. When breeding, the male (cock) feeds the female (hen) in the nest by regurgitating seed. When the eggs have hatched, the hen will feed her babies in the same way. If you buy more than one bird you will see them regularly regurgitating seed and feeding each other.

MOULTING

A budgie will moult its feathers several times a year – the main moult is usually in the autumn. You will usually find a few feathers on the bottom of the cage (which they often use as playthings), then lots of tiny feathers will be plucked out. In

Leg rings are fitted when a budgie is about 7-8 days old. They should be checked regularly to ensure they are not causing the bird any discomfort.

the main moult the loss of feathers can be considerable, but this is perfectly normal and the bird will soon grow new ones.

At the onset of the moult, budgies gradually shed and regrow the flight and tail feathers, as well as the small, body feathers. At this time they are particularly sensitive to draughts, so make sure that the cage is sited so that there is no possibility of draughts. If in doubt, put a light cover around the cage.

PREENING

Budgies preen each other, and so the single budgie will probably try to preen you – his adopted companion. The budgie will gently nibble at hair and eyebrows – ears are also a favourite. After the bird has finished preening you, it may lay its head down on your hand or lap and look up at you expectantly. What it is really saying is: "I have spent ages loving you – now its your turn!"

A budgie can preen its own feathers all over its body. It twists its little head and beak into the most amazing contortions to pick its feathers under and over its wings – but it cannot pick the top of its head. You can do this for your budgie, using your nail. The bird will sit still for ages, just moving its head for you to scratch at another spot.

During the moult, budgies lose

A budgie will often regurgitate seed for another bird in the cage.

and regrow their feathers, but at other times of the year they lose just a few of the tiny, down-like feathers. When the feathers re-grow, they have a sheath around them. Never be tempted to remove this sheath forcibly. As the feathers break through the skin, the budgie will pick off the sheath itself, bit by bit, in pieces so small that they just become dust. When the budgie lays down its head and waits for you to scratch its head, this is what it is asking you

to do. Of course, if you have more than one budgie, they will do this for each other, but, provided the birds are tame, they still enjoy having their heads scratched. Without knowing it, you will be slowly scratching away that irritating sheath.

DESTRUCTIVE BEHAVIOUR

Budgies in the wild start to breed as soon as the warm, rainy season arrives. They know that they will need water within the vicinity of the nest to feed their babies. Because water is always available in the cage, budgies in captivity can breed at any time. Fortunately, without a dark nesting box available, they will not start breeding.

However, budgies will instinctively gnaw at any wood, in the same way as their ancestors used to gnaw holes in the rotting trees to make nests. As the only wood available in the cage is the perches, budgies will often start to gnaw at them. Sometimes, in frustration, a budgie will tear away at the sand sheets and rip them to shreds.

This is something you just have to accept as the budgie is not misbehaving, being destructive in this way is part of a budgie's natural behaviour.

EGG LAYING

If you have chosen a female, or hen, budgie you will sometimes find an egg at the bottom of the cage, and the hen may spend a lot of time on the floor. If this happens, do not take the egg away, as this only encourages the hen to lay more eggs. Although laying eggs is a perfectly natural function, laying too many depletes the calcium in the bird. Just leave the egg or eggs in the cage, and put them back each time you clean it.

Sometimes a budgie may play football with the eggs, and will kick them around the cage. If an egg gets broken, it needs to be removed. After about two to three weeks, the egg laying cycle will be over. At this stage, you can remove the eggs, and it is unlikely that there will be another set for a considerable time.

RELATING TO PEOPLE

When you have a single budgerigar, it has no choice but to make you its companion.

Budgerigars were originally known as love birds, and there is no doubt that they do give and crave affection.

If a budgie does not have a companion to feed, it will regurgitate seed and give it to you. Sometimes a budgie may even try to give the seed to you by mouth, but mostly the bird will nibble away at your ear or the palm of your hand, and then feed it.

A single budgie often cannot understand why it cannot share your food, and will run down your arm and perch on a spoon trying to take a little of whatever it is you are eating. It is important to be careful here, because some of our food is not suitable for birds. We heard of one budgie who became addicted to a breakfast cereal, and while a tiny amount would not be harmful, filling up its little stomach so that it would not eat its own food was potentially disastrous.

Some budgies will try to drink out of the cup from which you are drinking.

Obviously, a budgie is not used to hot drinks, and the bird could scald its tongue, so it is better to discourage this habit. Needless to say, access to alcoholic drinks should also be prohibited.

5 Training Your Budgie

When you bring your budgie home for the first time, remember that it is feeling very strange. It is in a new cage, in a different environment, and among new people. It is bound to be nervous. You can help to give your budgie confidence by speaking softly and moving gently.

On the first day, give it a chance to settle down in its new home. Fill up the water fountain, and the seed and grit pots. Just for the first few days, scatter some seed on the floor of the cage so that, even if it is nervous about feeding from a new type of pot, there is still plenty of seed easily available. Make sure that you fit the mirror firmly in the cage.

HOLDING A BUDGIE

The correct way to hold a budgie is to enclose its body with one hand, holding its head with the thumb and forefinger at each side. When held this way, the bird cannot peck you. When a budgie is frightened or annoyed, its instinctive reaction is to peck, and that beak is strong and hard. If the budgie's head is held firmly, it cannot turn its head around to get the beak into pecking position.

The bird should be held firmly but gently, and this procedure should be practised so that you become confident in your handling, and the budgie learns to accept the restriction calmly. This

The correct way to hold a budgie.

is also important if you need to examine your budgie for any reason, or if you need to administer medication.

FINGER TRAINING

On the second day after arriving home, you can start to finger train your budgie. The more patience you can show at this stage, the more confident and tame the bird will eventually become. Start by opening the cage door with one hand, and blocking up the opening with the other. The last thing you want to happen is for the bird to escape, and to be chased around the room to be caught, when it is already feeling nervous.

PATIENCE IS A VIRTUE

Put one hand, containing a small piece of millet spray, into the cage, and hold the hand so that it can be easily reached from a perch. Keep the hand still for as long as you have the patience. After a while, the bird will usually nibble at the millet. Later you can repeat the exercise with a segment of sweet apple or carrot. The more time you are prepared to spend on this first 'making friends' exercise, the quicker your budgie will become tame, and, soon, it will

become affectionate too.

All the time you are finger training your pet, talk to it encouragingly, giving plenty of praise. Once you are able to put your hand into the cage without causing the bird to flutter around in fear, you can try to get it to perch on your finger. As it sits on the perch, put your finger under its chest and very gently press backwards, lifting it a little. To prevent itself from falling, the bird will step forward on to the next perch – which is, of course, your finger.

Once you have done this several times, your budgie will understand that when you put

Finger training requires patience.

your finger into the cage, you want it to jump on. Praise it for every new achievement. Instinct tells the bird when is is being praised. Now you have its trust – and if you have just the one budgie, you can start to train it to talk

SMALL TALK

Whether your budgie will learn to talk or not depends entirely on how much time you spend talking to it. There is no such thing as a 'talking strain' of budgie. Equally, it is not true that a male bird will

talk and a female will not. They are all mimics, but unless something is repeated again and again, they will not learn to mimic it.

One elderly lady, who was deaf and dumb, had a budgie with whom she spent all her time. The budgie could not learn to speak because he was never spoken to . However, the lady suffered very badly from asthma and had frequent bouts of severe coughing. Soon the budgie was coughing, and the noise was so frightening and realistic that he seemed to

Budgies will learn to talk, although training a single bird is easier.

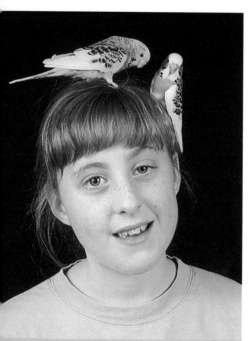

The more time you spend with your budgies, the tamer they will become.

THE BEST TEACHERS

Time and repetition is the only way to teach your budgie to talk. A child with a lot of patience, or a woman whose voice is higher than that of a man, are the best teachers.

Start first with a single word, repeat it again and again, and ask every member of the family to say the same word to the bird. The budgie's name is often the best word to start with – provided it is a relatively simple sound. Budgies seem unable to learn a word beginning with an 'H'.

It takes quite a while for the budgie to master the first word, but when it has, it seems to add to its vocabulary quite quickly. When the first breakthrough happens, it is a good idea to give a little tidbit and lots of praise. If you, or your child, has neither the time nor the patience to keep on repeating the same word or phrase again and again, another option is to make a tape of it and play the tape constantly to the budgie when the room he is in is quiet. With time and patience, a budgie can be taught to give its name and address – on many occasions, this has led to a joyful reunion of a lost pet and its owner.

have difficulty in hanging on to the perch when in the middle of an attack. Well-meaning budgie-breeding friends insisted that the lady should take the bird to the vet. Even the vet was nonplussed until, one day, the lady had an attack in his presence and the budgie joined in the terrible coughing. The budgie was, of course, as fit as a fiddle – mimicking the coughing was the only way he could communicate with his beloved owner.

JIMPY GOES TO SEA

One amazing true story was of a budgie which escaped and flew away from its home, which was near to the sea. Exhausted and hungry, it eventually found rest on the rigging of a ship and was rescued by a bird-loving sailor. Fortunately, the next port of call was only a few hours away. The sailor bought all the necessary supplies, and the budgie quickly became the ship's pet. To anyone who would listen, it chirped: "My name is Jimpy" and gave its address.

The sailor sent a letter from the next port of call, explaining the circumstances to the owner, and promised to bring back their pet when he was again in his home port. It was three months before Jimpy's ecstatic reunion with his real owner – who never again left a window open when Jimpy was out of his cage!

TRACING A LOST BIRD

Losing your beloved budgie can be a traumatic experience. If you are lucky enough to buy a bird with a closed, coded ring on its leg, the finder can often trace the bird. These rings have a code which is exclusive to one breeder, and, in the UK, the name and address of the breeder can be obtained from the Budgerigar Society. Other countries have similar arrangements in place.

STAR BUDGIES

Once you have taught your budgie to give its name and address, it can learn more and more phrases. Nursery rhymes, with their short lines and simple words, are often taught and cause a great deal of amusement. One budgie, a female, regularly brought tears of joy to her elderly owner as she sat on her glasses and gazed into her eyes saying: "Oh, I do love you!" She was, of course, only repeating something that she had heard on innumerable occasions.

FREE FLIGHT

A budgie should not be let out of its cage until it is finger tame. The bird needs to regard a finger as a safe landing place, something absolutely secure to hop on to when other things may be frightening. It is important to be patient and wait until the budgie has no fear of hands before letting it fly free for the first time. Once the budgie is out of its cage, it has to rely upon you to make the environment safe. Obviously, a budgie has no experience to draw on – and an ordinary living room can be fraught with dangers. For example, a glass window can be very dangerous.

When a budgie

If you allow your budgie to fly free, make sure the room is cleared of all possible hazards and escape routes.

first flies free, it panics when it finds that its usual perch has disappeared. It often flies around at great speed, trying to find somewhere it can land which is similar to the inside of its cage. It knows nothing about glass and can fly at the glass and hit it at great velocity, so great in fact that it can break its neck and kill itself. To a budgie, clear glass windows could mean just a wide open space to fly around freely.

THE FIRST OUTING

For your budgie's first outing, if there are net curtains, pull them almost shut, leaving just a few inches of space on the window-sill which it may well choose as its perch. Tops of pictures or mirrors are other favourite places to land for the first time. If there are no net curtains, pull the curtains shut and turn on the light. Needless to say, all windows and doors must be closed.

Consider every potential danger. An open fire must be closely guarded, but even a fireplace with no fire needs to be covered up, or a panicking bird could fly up the chimney and be too scared to come back down.

KEEPING STILL

Sometimes, happily, the first perch the frightened bird chooses is a head or shoulder. If this happens, keep quite still – a sudden hand movement could frighten your budgie away. If the bird can learn that people are the safest landing spot, this is a great step forward. Keep still and let your budgie explore. It will often nibble at ears, bury itself in long hair, and then walk down the arm and find the familiar finger to sit on. When your budgie feels safe with you or a member of your family, you have won half the battle of training.

If you have two budgies, one will often be less timid than the other. However, the shy budgie will often take a lead from its bolder companion, and will learn that people should be regarded as friends.

OTHER PETS

Other pets can be a danger to new budgies. Although there are many cases of budgies and cats becoming the best of friends, this is the exception – not the rule. On your budgie's first outings, make sure that both cats and dogs are banned from the room until the bird is safely back in the cage.

TAKE OUT THE PLANTS

Once a budgie begins to explore the room, greenery becomes a lure. In no time, a precious potted plant will be shredded by a playful budgie. It is bad enough losing a plant, but some house plants are poisonous to birds, so it is better to play safe and remove all plants when your budgie is flying loose.

RETURNING TO THE CAGE

When your budgie has experienced its first free flight, you will then want the bird to return to the cage. More patience is needed here. The bird is now finger trained, so go towards it and gently hold out a finger. Usually, the budgie will hop on. Steadily and without jerking your finger, walk back to the cage and place your hand, with the budgie, back into the cage. Once the bird is inside, use the other hand to cover the entrance while you transfer the budgie on to a wooden perch. Finally, withdraw your hand and close the door.

Sometimes this does not work quite so smoothly. The budgie will sit on your finger as you walk gently towards the cage then, just as you put your finger down towards the cage door, off flies the budgie, back to the windowsill,

picture frame or whatever new perch it fancies. You try again, and again. People laugh at 'bird brains', but you will soon find that budgies can be quite intelligent. It does not take more than a few seconds for a budgie to realise that being carried back to the cage means the end of freedom. When the bird decides it does not want to go back into the cage it is surprising how stubborn it can be. Yet again, the answer is patience. The budgie can play its 'bid for

Your budgie can be taught to perch on the rim of a cup – but make sure it does not contain a hot drink.

freedom game' for a long time before it eventually agrees to return to its own home and have a feed.

number of occasions, the budgie will realise that it cannot win, and will allow itself to be carried back to the cage on a finger.

THE LAST RESORT

There are some occasions – perhaps when you are going out, or last thing at night when you are going to bed – when there is no alternative but to return the bird to the cage against its will. Chasing your budgie until it is exhausted can undo all the trust that patient training has instilled, so you need to have a more effective plan of campaign.

The first step is to switch on the light and pull the curtains to make the room light-proof. Position one person where they can see exactly where the budgie is perched, and another at the light switch. The person at the light switch turns off the light, plunging the room into darkness, and at the same moment the other person picks up the budgie, who cannot see to fly. The poor budgie must then be held firmly, and returned – rather ignominiously – to the cage. You will find that if this procedure is repeated on a

Health Care

In general, budgies are healthy little birds and suffer from few diseases. However, things can go wrong, and nothing is more upsetting than seeing your budgie ill and not knowing what to do. Some of the possible mishaps which could occur are listed below, along with the appropriate treatment programmes to follow.

MINOR INJURIES

Budgies are playful and inquisitive creatures and, occasionally, they can injure themselves. Usually this happens when the budgie picks at something in the cage which has a sharp point – a clip holding a millet spray or piece of cuttle-fish, for example.

If the bird sustains a small cut which is bleeding, this can often be stopped with a styptic pencil. The budgie should be kept as still as possible until the bleeding has stopped, and then the wound can be treated exactly as you would a cut that you had sustained. It is also a good idea to apply a mild antiseptic–analgesic ointment is recommended. Try talking to your budgie and holding its attention in order to prevent it from picking at the wound.

If a small wound should become infected, it can cause a tiny ulcer to form. This should be painted twice a day with tincture of iodine, and the abscess will generally disappear. However, if the infection continues, a vet will supply some antibiotic ointment which should quickly clear it up.

FRACTURES

Legs or wings can be broken in accidents in the home. In most cases, the fracture can be mended, but this is definitely a case for the vet.

TREATING A SICK BUDGIE

No matter what the illness, providing a warm environment is essential. If your bird is kept in a centrally-heated room, the addition of a light cover around the cage is all that is necessary. However, if your budgie lives in a relatively cool room, it should be moved. The ideal temperature is 29 degrees Centigrade (85 degrees Fahrenheit). If you place an open dish of water near the cage it will help to give more humidity to the air.

After any illness, it is good practice to put a few drops of liquid Vitamin B12, (available from pharmacies) into the drinking fountain for a few days. This is an essential vitamin for budgerigars. The normal source of supply is from their own dried-up droppings, but during the course of an illness this source may be depleted because of the need to keep the cage scrupulously clean. Alternatively, a few drops of another type of pleasant-tasting multivitamin liquid can be given.

Sick budgies can be treated just like sick babies, but it must be remembered that, whereas a baby will weigh quite a few pounds, a budgie weighs about two ounces, so the quantity of any medication must be cut down or diluted immensely.

COUGHS AND COLDS

A bird with a cough or cold is very much like a child with a cold. The symptoms are similar: the nostrils exude mucus, the eyes

This budgie combines the spangle and yellowface varieties, making a very attractive bird.

sometimes run, the breathing is wheezy and the bird looks fluffed up and sorry for itself. The treatment is the same as that for a child. Keep it warm. A few drops of pleasant-tasting cough mixture in the water fountain helps the congestion, as does a container of mentholated rub in hot water near the cage.

TRICHOMONIASIS

If your budgie suffers prolonged and violent vomiting, consult your vet. This can often be sign of a disease called trichomoniasis. It can be treated with a tiny amount of Emtryl (known as Trykil in the US), but this should not be administered by an amateur.

MITES

Although your bird/birds may have no contact with any other birds, very rarely they can be infected with mites. These tiny parasites feast on the blood of wild birds and can be carried into a house on the wings of flies. During the day, the mites are grey in colour and hide in cracks and crevices underneath the seed pots or the floor covering. At night they emerge to gorge on the bird's blood – and the red, blood-filled creatures rapidly increase in

number. They can sometimes be seen when a light is turned on in the morning, or when a cover is taken off the cage.

There are other forms of mites, such as feather mite and fodder mite, but these are very rarely found among pet birds. Should any mite be found, or if they are suspected due to frantic scratching, both birds and cage should be sprayed with a safe preparation containing hexachloride, malathion or derris root.

SCALY FACE

The only other mite likely to infect a bird through transport on flies is scaly face. It is exceedingly rare that pet birds are affected but cases have been known. At least when this mite attacks, the effects are visual and can be dealt with. The mites burrow into the beak, eyelids or legs of the bird creating a huge number of tiny tunnels.

The irritation causes the bird to exude a sticky liquid. The skin debris caused by the burrowing of the mite sticks to this liquid, and it sets as a crust. The beak, eyes or legs, whichever is affected, is covered with this scale – hence the name. It can be cured, slowly, by covering the scale with sulphur

White and blue have combined to produce this delicate colour.

ointment or Vaseline, which cuts off the air to the tunnels and gradually kills the mite.

A quicker method is to dose the bird with a tiny amount of Ivermectin which has been diluted 100 times. Again, this should be administered only by a vet.

WORMS
The same dilution of Ivermectin (100 times) will also kill all worms. Unless these are present when the birds are purchased, or are brought in by another new acquisition, worms are unlikely to be found in a pet bird. The main source of contamination is from wild birds perching on the wires of an aviary – the worm eggs are carried in their droppings. The symptoms of worm infestation are loose droppings, lethargy and loss of weight.

INFLAMED EYES
Just like us, a bird can get something in its eye. In the budgie's case, this is usually a seed husk. In an effort to clear it, the budgie rubs its eye on the perch or tries to scratch at it. This can cause the eye to become very sore and inflamed.

You can help your budgie very easily by using a diluted eye lotion (roughly 50 per cent water to 50 per cent eye lotion). Fill half an eye-bath, or some other small container, with the liquid. Soak a piece of cotton-wool in water and squeeze it out, then soak it in the eye lotion solution. Hold the bird on its side and allow the liquid to dribble from the cotton-wool into its eye. If the eye is already inflamed, continue to give this treatment several times a day, for a few days, until the eye is clear and healthy again. A speck of golden eye ointment around the eyelids can also be soothing.

VOMITING

Regurgitating food should not be confused with vomiting. When a budgie vomits, it throws up seeds violently – not like the gentle action of regurgitation. When a budgie vomits it flicks the seed away forcibly, and very often the seed lands up on top of its head. The head can become sticky and the feathers congested. The feathers around the base of the beak may become sticky with mucus. This is often because the bird has eaten something which does not agree with it, or the food may have been contaminated.

But sometimes it can be a symptom of a more serious complaint.

Although budgies are usually very healthy little creatures, they do not have not a great deal of stamina to endure illness. As an emergency measure, the water can be replaced with cold tea, which often settles an upset tummy. However, if the vomiting continues for more than a day, it is best to seek the advice of a vet or an experienced budgerigar breeder.

To make the cold tea, first use a tea-bag to make a cup of tea. Then take the once-used teabag and make another strong cup. Let the second cup get cold and use this to fill the water fountain.

Breeding Budgies

In many cases, budgie owners start with one or two pet birds, and then they become increasingly fascinated by their hobby, and decide to try to breed. As they see the first egg laid and then hatched, as they watch the tiny scrap of flesh turn into the most beautiful bird, with limpid, trusting black eyes, the budgie bug bites – and they are hooked for the rest of their lives. They become budgie fanciers, a special breed of people whose lives revolve around their budgerigars.

Most budgie breeders build a birdroom or an aviary, and many join the local bird club, where there are friendly, experienced fanciers who are willing to help newcomers to build and equip their aviaries, and to give general advice.

BREEDING STOCK

Before beginning to breed with a pair of budgies, you must make sure that they are of breeding age.

A hen is not considered fully mature until she is 10-11 months old. If she starts to lay eggs earlier, there could be problems, such as egg binding, which could render her unable to breed for the rest of her life. A cock should be at least 10 months old before facing the rigours of raising his first family.

THE BREEDING CAGE

The first requirement when breeding budgies, even if you only have one pair, is a breeding cage. Ideally, one cage is needed for each breeding pair. Breeding cages can be purchased ready-made from a pet shop, or they can be constructed very simply. Basically, a breeding cage is a wooden box with a wire front.

When starting breeding, the breeding cage can be positioned almost anywhere. Some of the most experienced and successful breeders of today tell stories about their first breeding cage being kept on the landing, on the wall of the laundry room, and other unlikely locations! However, the main considerations when siting your first breeding cage or cages, are the health and comfort of the birds, and the convenience of the owner for cleaning and inspecting purposes.

A garage is unsuitable if a car is to be started up inside, as the fumes are poisonous to birds. The laundry room may not be a good idea if there is a lot of steam in the atmosphere. Locating a cage too high can make cleaning and inspecting too difficult for the breeder. So, remember, a little thought in advance can prevent difficulties later on.

THE DIMENSIONS

The minimum size for a single breeding cage is 75cm wide x 45cm high x 30cm deep. When the top, base, sides and back have been put together, a board placed across the front prevents husks and other debris falling to the floor. From the point of view of cleanliness and attractiveness, it is recommended that the inside of the cage is painted with white or a pale-coloured emulsion paint.

There are several different types of breeding cage fronts. It is best to purchase one before the cage is made to ensure a good fit. The best type has a large access door in the centre. This enables the

breeder to catch the birds more easily – and when four or five young chicks are flying in the cage, it is a very different matter from putting in a finger for a tame bird to use as a perch.

Two timber perches, preferably 2cm x 1.5cm, have to be fixed in the cage. The best position is about 10cm from each side. To fix the perches, a slit should be made in the front of the perch. This is slid over one of the wires of the front, and the tension holds it against the back wall of the cage.

BEDDING

A thick layer of clean wood-shavings, which have not been contaminated by chemicals or vermin, is the best covering for the floor. These will make the cage easier to clean when the hen begins to excrete the copious droppings prior to egg laying. In fact, she continues to drop copiously throughout the period that the eggs – and the chicks – are in the nest. The shavings also act as a cushion when the babies first come out of the nest, sometimes falling in the process.

NESTBOX

The next necessity is a nestbox. Again, budgies are accommodating. When budgies were first introduced into the UK, the breeders supplied hollowed-out coconut shells, with a hole for access drilled into them. In one case, two pet budgies were given the freedom of a spare bedroom and they worked out their own solution. They hollowed out their own nest in the plaster behind the window curtains. There, the hen laid her eggs and they brought up their babies quite happily.

For the comfort of the birds, for safety and ease of access, the best type of nestbox is one made from plywood or softwood. Softwood is the better of the two, particularly the type used for floorboards, as it helps to absorb moisture when the chicks are growing and has good insulating properties which help to keep the nestbox warm. The hen can chew at the box with no fear that she might eat the glue, which can happen when plywood is used.

The ideal size for the nestbox is 30cm x 22cm x 17cm externally. No great carpentry skills are necessary to construct one of these nestboxes, it just needs to be dark inside, and secure. This is a little room for the hen, a room in which she will spend many hours at a stretch, sitting on her eggs or

A violet spangle hen – hens are not considered fully mature until they are 10-11 months of age.

and front, two pieces 30cm x 15cm for the top and bottom, and two side pieces of 17cm x 15cm. The box may be positioned inside the cage, fixed to the back wall, or hung on the outside of the cage. If the box is hung on the outside, it gives more room inside the cage, and gives much easier access for the breeder. This is very important when the chicks have to be inspected.

If the box is to be hung on the front of the cage, a hole of about two inches square should be cut out of the cage front, about 5cms above a perch. A round entrance hole, about 4cm diameter must be cut in the back of the nestbox. Nail together the back, bottom and sides. Now cut the front panel into two pieces, approximately 13cm from the top, and fix hinges to the outside. This will enable the top half to be dropped for inspection. The top can be fastened with a luggage clasp. Two screw eyes, one at each end of the back of the box, are hung on to two screws on the outside front of the breeding cage. Drill two or three 10mm holes high up on each end to provide ventilation.

Nestboxes are usually painted with emulsion paint or varnished on the outside, but the inside

sleeping. She must, therefore, feel absolutely secure.

To make a simple nestbox with a let-down front, cut two pieces of board, 30cm x 22cm for the back

In the wild, budgies lay their eggs in a hollow they make from a rotting tree. In captivity, a nesting box must be provided.

must be left unpainted as the hen, and possibly the babies, will eat the wood. The box should be half-filled with clean, uncontaminated sawdust.

CHOOSING THE RIGHT TIME

The next thing to decide is when to start trying to breed the birds for the first time. Budgies are very accommodating and will start to breed at almost any time of the year, provided they are in a really fit state of health. When they have started to moult feathers is certainly not a good time – you must wait until the moult is over.

Once the budgies begin to breed, they will usually be in the breeding cage for about three months. During this time, the hen will occupy the nestbox for long periods. Too much heat can make this very uncomfortable for her, so, therefore, the beginning of summer is not a good time to start breeding. The best time for the absolute beginner to try breeding is in the early Spring – the same time as wild birds. However, if the breeding cage is to be sited where there is a small amount of heating in the house, then the budgies will breed during the winter months. When the birds are ready for breeding, they exhibit their breeding fitness. The cock is very active and lively, and will be seen chasing the hen. The hen will be even more destructive than usual, ripping up paper, gnawing at wood, and possibly tearing up the sand sheet in her cage.

FEEDING THE BREEDING PAIR

The food dishes should be positioned in the centre of the cage where they will not be fouled by droppings. During the breeding process, in addition to seed, grit and cuttle-fish, a little soft-food should be supplied to the birds – just a dessertspoon per pair, per day. There are several budgie soft-foods available in pet stores, or you can make your own and keep it in the fridge.

This can be done by taking a thick slice (about 2 oz) of wholemeal bread and making it into breadcrumbs in a food processor. Dry off the breadcrumbs in a cooker after it has been used and then turned off, or in any warm place. Put the dried breadcrumbs back into the food processor and re-process. This turns them into much finer crumbs. Now add a medium-sized carrot and a hard-boiled egg (including shell) and process until the mixture is fine in texture.

SIGNS OF EGG LAYING

Up to this point, the preparations for breeding are the same for both cock and hen. Needless to say, it is of utmost importance that you now put one cock and one hen into each breeding cage. This advice may seem unnecessary, but the stories of breeders waiting endlessly with no results – and then finding that the birds in the cage were both of the same sex – are legion.

Generally, about seven or eight days after the pair is put into the breeding cage, the hen's droppings will begin to become softer and more copious. This is a sign of egg laying. If, after two weeks, there is no sign of egg laying and no eggs are laid, it may be because there are no other budgies around. Budgies are gregarious creatures and breed better when there is other budgie noise around. If the breeding cage is in a position where it would not disturb the rest of the household, try leaving a radio on near the cage. Budgies like loud music, and they do not seem to be fussy about what kind it is – they accept anything from hard rock to the classics!

INSPECTING THE EGGS

Once you have detected signs of egg laying, gently tap on the nestbox each day. This is almost like the way in which we knock at a door before entering. Remember, the nestbox is your budgie's home now. You are the intruder. Sometimes when you tap on the box, the hen will emerge from the nestbox into the cage. Sometimes, particularly if she is very tame, she will remain in the box sitting, even when you gently let down the front-flap and look in.

If the hen does not move, gently lift her chest far enough to see underneath her to check if she has laid an egg. If she has, make a note of the date the egg was laid. If you particularly want to, you can mark the egg with a soft, water-soluble marker. Generally, it is not a good idea to handle and mark eggs. This is because it is easy to damage the eggs as you handle them. Equally important is the fact that the eggs are porous, and any bacteria on your hands could be rubbed off on to the egg and absorbed, killing the developing chick. However, it is a temptation for a beginner to mark the eggs so that they can check upon their progress.

Once the first egg is laid, a new egg will be laid every other day until the clutch is complete. Four or five eggs is the normal number, but a clutch as large as 18 eggs has been known. The eggs usually take 18 days to hatch after being laid. This means that the first baby in a normal five-egg clutch will be ten days old before the final chick is hatched – and, as you will see, the eldest will look like a little monster in comparison with its newly-hatched brother or sister.

THE BABIES

When they are first hatched, the babies are completely naked, with no feathers at all. The eyes are closed, the head is large in comparison to the body, and the neck is so thin that it seems incapable of holding the large head. As soon as the chick is hatched, the mother starts to try to feed it and, very soon, it will have a creamy blob inside the transparent stomach.

Once the clutch of eggs is complete, the less you disturb the nestbox the better. Every morning, tap the box and gently open the flap, just to ensure the hen is in good health. On the eighteenth day after the first egg is laid, when you check the hen, also check to see if the egg has hatched. This is usually obvious as soon as you open the box, as you will see the two halves of the empty shell. Do not interfere with the shell. The mother will either throw it out or eat it. Check again, after a couple of hours, to make sure that the little creamy blob of food is in the tummy, which indicates that the mother is feeding the baby.

If the chick's stomach appears flat and empty, you have a problem because it cannot survive for long without food. One solution is to foster the baby into another nest where the mother is feeding well – but the chances are that you will not have another nest ready for it. In this situation, all that you can do is to hold the tiny little scrap in a warm hand, and with a pipette, a cotton bud, or even a matchstick with the head broken off, drop one or two drops of warm milk into the beak. You

This little chick has just broken out of its shell.

will see the tiny drop in the chick's stomach. Put the chick back under its mother and check again in a couple of hours. Usually, after you have done this once or twice, the mother realises what is needed and will begin to feed her baby herself. Once she is feeding the first baby, there should be no further problems when the next egg hatches.

THE DEVELOPING CHICKS
The golden rule is to regard the nestbox as the hen's home. You are the intruder, and, therefore, you must interfere as little as possible. Confine yourself to checking once a day – morning is best – to make sure that the family is thriving. Once a week, remove the top, soiled sawdust and put in a handful of clean sawdust. When you remove the chicks to do this, make sure that your hands are warm. Put the chicks in a bowl, lined with sawdust, which must also be warm, and try to keep them out for as short a period as possible. It takes only a minute to remove a small handful of sawdust and replace it with clean.

A handful of baby budgies at three weeks of age.

When the oldest chick is about four weeks old, it may leave the nest and play in the sawdust on the bottom of the breeding cage. It is wise to have a small, shallow, wooden box, rather like a three-sided box with a lid, open at the front, in the bottom of the cage – preferably somewhere towards the back. Sometimes the chicks make such a nuisance of themselves by pestering the cock for seed or for attention, the cock may lose his temper and decide to discipline them. Some cocks can be quite vicious and may even injure the chicks. If the chicks have a little home to play in, it obviates any domestic upheaval.

DECISION TIME

Once all the chicks have left the nestbox, all the soiled sawdust needs to be cleared out – and then you have a decision to make. If you leave the nestbox on the cage with the mother and father in the cage, it will be no time before you find that the hen has started to lay eggs again. If this is what you want,

If you want to breed budgies, Serious consideration must be given to providing the right environment.

In this budgie, two varieties have been combined to give a yellowface bird with a crest which looks like a fringe.

has already started to lay eggs, these should also be removed. The pair should be left in the breeding cage for a week or so before transferring them back to their pet cage or the garden aviary.

PARTING

When the chicks are about six weeks old, they should be parted from their parents and housed, either in a stock cage, which is exactly like a breeding cage without a nestbox, or in a large pet cage. If you intend to sell the chicks as pets, or to give them to friends or family members, finger training can start from the moment they leave the nestbox.

Often, when a breeder sees that first nest of chicks, with their round, trusting eyes, and watches the transformation from nakedness to a covering of the softest coloured feathers, he or she is hooked – and wants to continue to breed budgies. If this is the case, serious thought must be given to providing a proper home for the stock. A cage in the bedroom is fine for pet budgies,

the nestbox needs to be refilled, half-full, with fresh, clean sawdust. If you do not wish to continue breeding, the nestbox should be removed from the cage. If the hen

Once you start breeding budgies, it becomes an increasingly fascinating and complex hobby. The bird on the right shows the strange effect of adding the grey factor. In the green series it just changes the shade of a green bird, but if the bird is blue, the factor completely covers the blue and the budgie appears grey.

or for your first experiment in breeding budgies, but if a number of cages are going to be used, on a permanent basis, then thought has to be given to providing a birdroom.

There are many different types of birdrooms, as well as numerous requirements covering safety, ventilation, insulation and equipment, so it would be advisable to read a detailed, specialised book on breeding, so you can find out the financial outlay that is required.

FAMILY PLANNING

Whatever your future plans may be, your first breeding pair should only be allowed to raise one more clutch of chicks within the year. Left to their own devices, a pair of budgies will continue to lay eggs and rear chicks while there is a nestbox and food available. But laying too many eggs depletes the hen's supply of calcium, and feeding the young brood really takes it out of the father. Two rounds of breeding per year is as much as should be allowed, and the rest of the time should be given over to rest and exercise.